Colorful Illusions

Tricks to Fool Your Eyes

Aki Nurosi

with Mark Shulman

Sterling Publishing Co., Inc.

New York

Colorful Illusions
Produced by Orange Avenue, Inc.
San Francisco, CA

Creative Direction
Hallie Warshaw and Aki Nurosi

Illusion Art
Aki Nurosi

Text
Mark Shulman and Aki Nurosi

Production
Doug Popovich

Library of Congress Cataloging-in-Publication Data Available
10 9 8 7 6 5 4 3 2 1

Published by Sterling Publishing Company, Inc.
387 Park Avenue South, New York, NY 10016

© 2000 Aki Nurosi and Mark Shulman

Created and produced by Orange Avenue, Inc.
275 Fifth Street, San Francisco, CA 94103, USA

Distributed in Canada by Sterling Publishing Co., Inc.
c/o Canadian Manda Group, One Atlantic Avenue, Suite 105
Toronto, Ontario, Canada M6K 3E7

Distributed in Great Britain and Europe by Chris Lloyd
463 Ashley Road, Parkstone, Poole, Dorset
BH14 0AX, England

Distributed in Australia by Capricorn Link (Australia) Pty Ltd.
P.O. Box 6651, Baulkham Hills, Business Centre
NSW 2153, Australia

Printed in China.

Sterling ISBN 0-8069-2997-9 Trade
         ISBN 0-8069-6097-3 Paper

Created by
Orange Avenue
Making Creative Products for Growing Minds
San Francisco, CA

About the Authors

Aki Nurosi is a professor of graphic design at the Rhode Island School of Design.

Since childhood, she has been attracted to the brilliant colors of nature. This has led to her lifelong exploration of the impact of color, in her graphic designs and her research. Aki received her Bachelor of Arts degree from the *École Superieure des Arts Modernes* in Paris and her Master of Fine Arts degree, specializing in graphic design, from Yale University.

Aki's university professors encouraged her to one day teach others. Her teaching concentrates on the subject of color and how it is applied in design. In 1994, Aki presented a paper to the Conference on Color Education held at UIAH, the university of art and design in Helsinki, Finland.

Her artworks have been exhibited in numerous galleries, and she maintains an active color consulting practice in Providence, Rhode Island, where she lives with her husband Hammett. Aki has a contrasting cat named Serendipity (it's black and white) and a Manx cat whose gorgeous coloring earned him the name Harmony. What color is the Manx? You'll find the answer in this book.

Mark Shulman writes for children and adults.

He was an early reader, an uncle at eight years old, a camp counselor, a radio newscaster, a New York City tour guide, and an advertising creative director before writing this book. He has since learned a lot about color illusions from Aki.

Mark is a graduate of the University of Buffalo. He and his wife Kara live in New York.

To the trust in HARMONY

Acknowledgments

My sincere and deep gratitude to:
Hammett, who has always been there helping me overcome my fears,
my teacher Professor Armin Hofmann, who awakened the passion for color in me
and encouraged me to teach it,
Hallie, my dedicated and caring student and friend of more than a decade, who
brought this project to existence,
and Mark, whose writing made the text sensible and more fun to read.
—Aki Nurosi

For my wife, my family, and all the friends
who could not fit up there with me at my wedding.
—Mark Shulman

The authors and producers also wish to thank the following people:
Charles Nurnberg, Sheila Barry, Doug Popovich, Robyn Brode, Tanya Napier, Robert Warshaw, Elaine Warshaw,
and Kara Pranikoff.

TABLE OF CONTENTS

How to get the most out of this book

- Look at each picture or illusion before you read
  the questions.

- Give the colors and shapes enough time to make an impact.

- Think about the effect each illusion is having on you.

- Read the questions beside each illusion.

- Look in the back of the book (starting on page 66)
  for the answers.

- Consult pages 78 and 79 for explanations of words
  and ideas related to color.

- Flip the pages . . . but don't flip out!

Colorful Illusions

About color and illusions

In order to use color effectively it is necessary to recognize that color deceives continually.

—Josef Albers,
artist and teacher

Imagine—today's your day.

You're in an expensive automobile showroom, shopping for a sports car. You know which car you want. You just have to choose the color. White seems quiet. Black looks mysterious. Your eye keeps coming back to the red one. But do you know why? Because red looks *fast*.

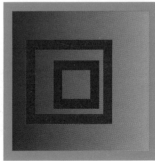

Red means go

Why red? As colors go, red is always the first to catch the eye. That's why it sits at the top of the rainbow. And that's why you're sitting in your new red sports car. Now imagine you're driving down the highway. The top is down. You're feeling good, until you see red—the flashing lights of a police car. You were going no faster than the other cars. Why did you get a speeding ticket? Because red looks *fast*.

Welcome to the world of color illusions. It's true that the police stop more red cars than any other color. It's also true that yellow makes objects look larger—the perfect color for warning signs.

And it's true that black objects look smaller. Black is the absence of color; it swallows up light. With less light, you get the illusion of less size.

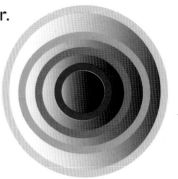

Why you see what you see

There are two main reasons why colors can trick you: the way vision works and the way light works. Your eyes send information to your brain, which adapts to make sense of whatever it sees...no matter how strange. And then there's light. Without light, there *is* no color. When you say something has color, you're actually describing a reflection of the light falling on it. Change the light, and presto! You change the color.

Is seeing believing? Everything you see is a kind of illusion. You think you see one thing, but you're actually seeing *a number of things* all at once—a random assortment of different colors and levels of brightness. But your mind tricks you into organizing those things into groups…whether they belong there or not.

There's illusion in store for you

Let's take a trip to the grocery store. At the meat counter, the red meat is surrounded with green decorations. The green makes the red look redder, so the meat looks fresher. When you take the meat home, it may not look as good. You've just experienced the afterimage effect, one of the phenomena this book explores.

Grocery stores are full of color illusions. Take a look next time. Carrots look more orange when

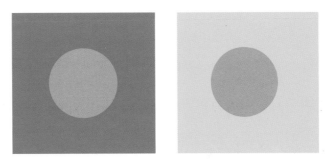

there's green or blue on the bags. Potatoes inside purple-tinted sacks seem more yellow, and better looking. And a blue background helps oranges really live up to their name. These are all examples of the afterimage effect. By controlling what your eyes see, the grocer helps you fill your cart.

Artful color illusions

Most of the pictures in this book are optical illusions based on color. They're meant to affect your mind as well as your senses.

 You'll see simple interactions between shapes and colors, as well as complex ones. Sometimes you'll perceive these shapes and colors separately, sometimes all at once.

Although the examples in this book are two dimensional and stationary, you may perceive many of them as three dimensional, and in some you may even experience movement. Just take your time and let each illusion happen to you.

See it your way

No one else has the same brain you've got. No one else has seen everything you've seen. That's why each example may seem different to you than to other people. Since perception involves interaction, go ahead and really look at each illusion. Interact with it. Turn it over in your mind. Then draw your own conclusions.

We hope this book will provide you with some understanding of color and form—how they interact, and how they can affect you. Sometimes seeing is believing. Sometimes it isn't.

See for yourself!

Narrow Arrows

Do the arrows point up, like rooftops,
or down, like open books?

If you look at the illusion long enough,
do the arrows appear to shift direction?

What's happening?
See page 66.

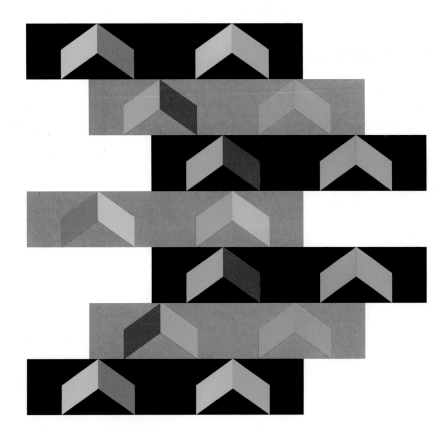

True Blue?

Are the blue bars in Figure A and Figure B the same color?

What's happening?
See page 66.

Figure A

Figure B

3 Sides, 3 Corners, 3D

Could these triangles actually be built in 3D?

What happens when they convert to full color?

Do they appear to be tumbling?

What's happening?
See page 67.

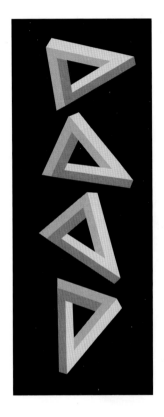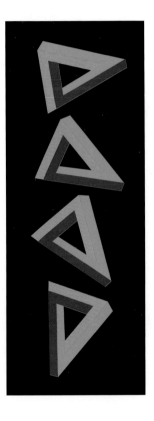

TV Dinner

Does the orange background change color in the middle or stay the same?

How many kinds of shapes are on this page?

What's happening?
See page 67.

Dots and Diamonds

Each black diamond has five rings with five center dots.

In Figure A, are the five center dots different colors, mixed, or all the same?

Is that also true in Figure B?

How many of the center dots match the dot outside the diamond?

What's happening?
See page 68.

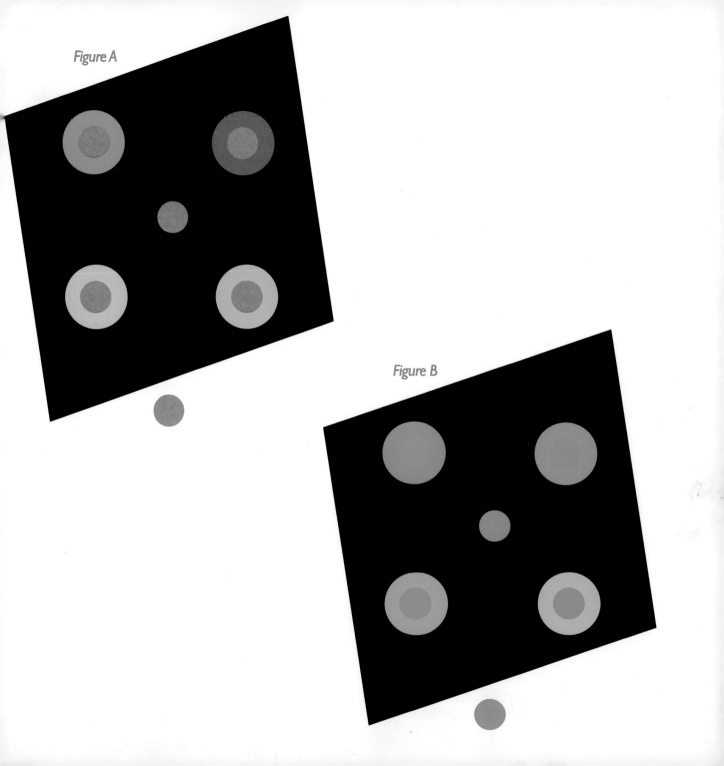

Figure A

Figure B

Dandelions

Look at each pair of dandelions up close.

Now step back a few feet and look at each double dandelion, maybe even squint at them.

What do each of the double dandelions appear to do?

What's happening?

See page 68.

Stick Matches

How many gray sticks are on this page?

What's happening?

See page 69.

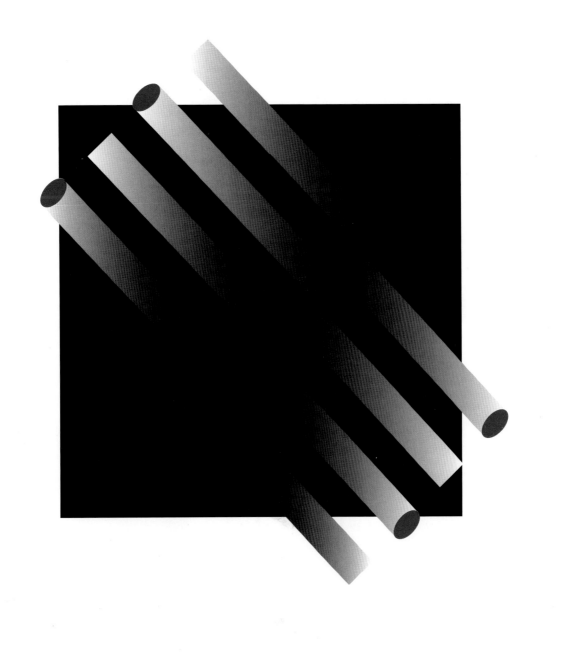

Wavy Groovy

How many of the horizontal bars are wavy?

How many are straight?

Which color bars look the most wavy?

What's happening?
See page 69.

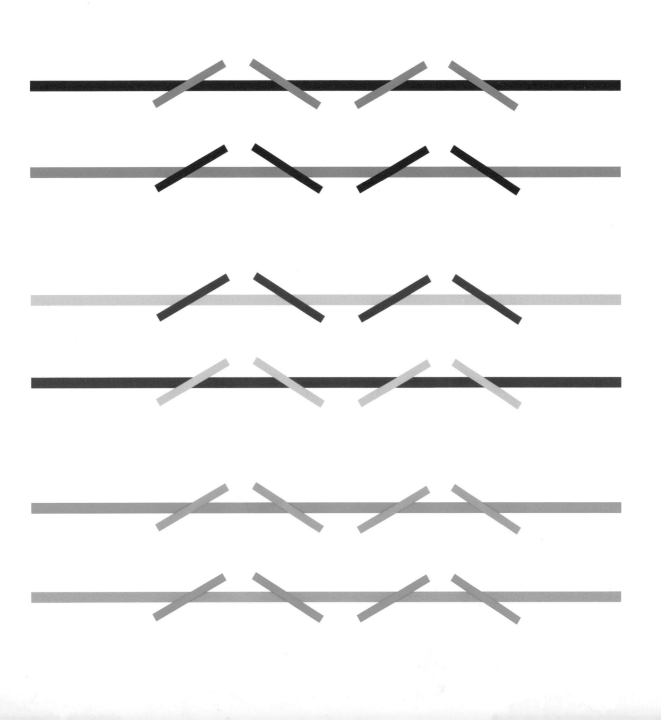

Whirly Swirly

Are the outside circles in Figure A the same distance from each other?

Are the circles in Figure B also the same distance apart?

Are all the largest and smallest circles actually circles?

Are Figures A and B each having a different effect?

What's happening?
See page 70.

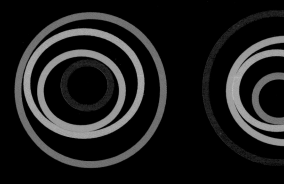

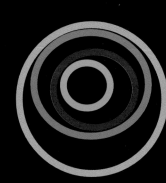

Figure A

Figure B

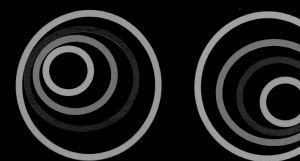

Box of Dots

Look closely at each pair of squares.

Which pairs have dots that match in the middle?

Which pairs don't?

What's happening?
See page 70.

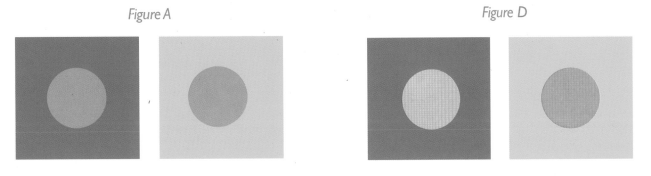

Figure A

Figure D

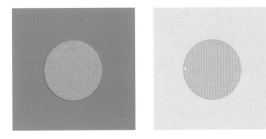

Figure B

Figure E

Figure C

Figure F

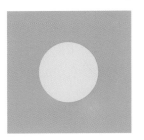

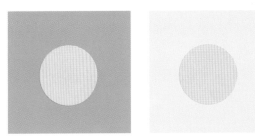

White Triangles

How many squares do you see in each figure?

How many large triangles do you see in each figure?

Which are on top, the white triangles or the colored ones?

Do each of the white triangles appear to have the same brightness?

What's happening?
See page 71.

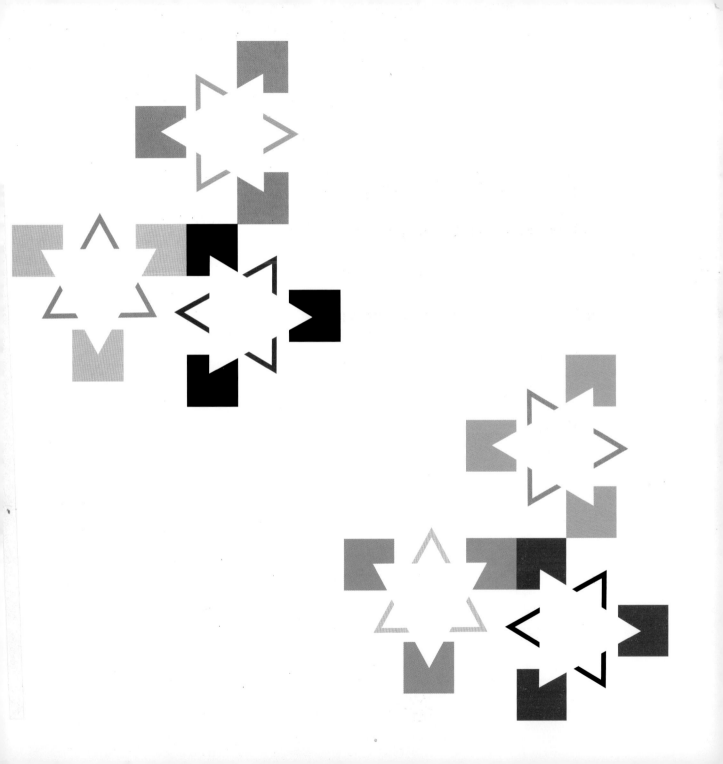

Bars and Stripes Forever

How many transparent bars do you see?

How many white bars do you see?

Which bars are in front: blue, transparent, or white?

What's happening?

See page 71.

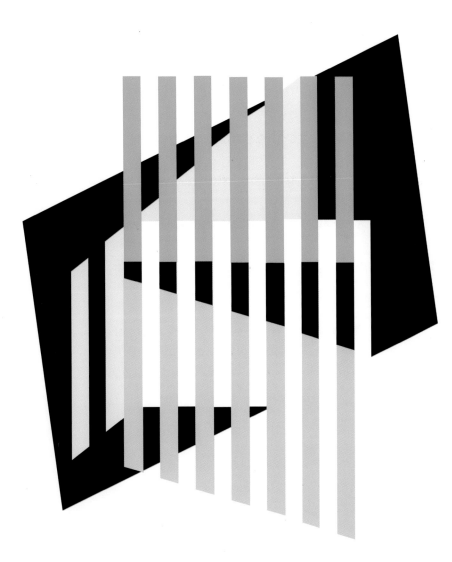

Red Grill

Are the green boxes all the same, or do they change color?

Are the red lines all the same, or do they change color?

What do you see at the points where the red lines cross?

All in all, do you see red on green or green on red?

What's happening?
See page 72.

Fact Checkers

Look at the small vertical lines in the black and red fields.

Are they all the same width?

When you compare the two fields, are the small lines the same color?

What's happening?
See page 72.

Dashing Dots

Which line of dots has more space between dots—
the blue one or the red one?

Which line is actually longer?

What's happening?
See page 73.

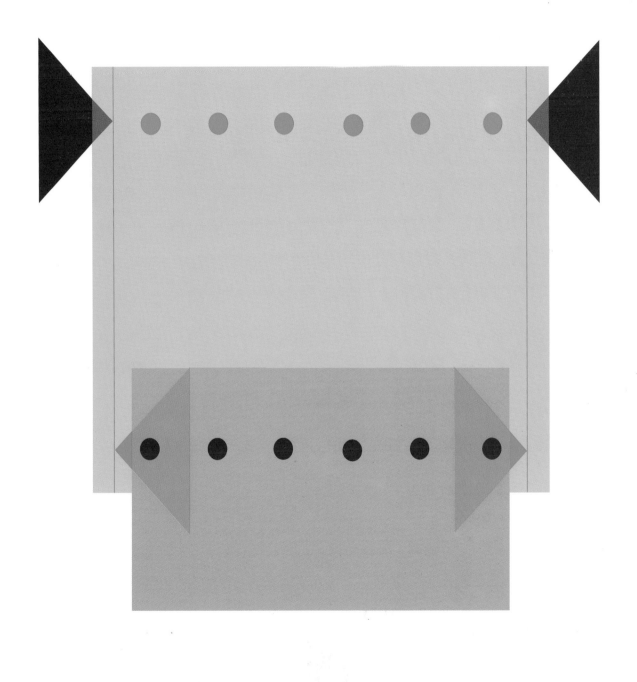

Mountains by Satellite

Each large circle has three smaller rings inside it.

Compare the inside rings to their neighbors.

Are all the second-largest rings the same size?
The second-smallest? The smallest?

Do these figures look like mountains seen
from directly above?

Do they seem to be the same height?

Do they appear to be in motion?

What's happening?
See page 73.

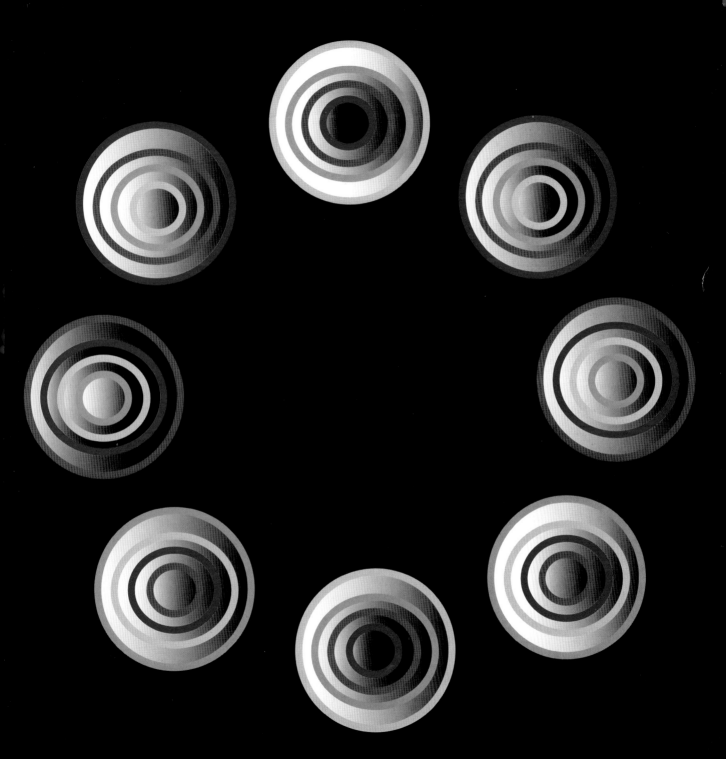

Stilts Tilts

Are all the vertical lines parallel?

Are they straight or wavy?

What's happening?
See page 74.

Crazy Eights

Which is larger, the outer ring of each smaller circle or the inner ring of each larger circle?

Is the larger pair of circles the same size?

Is the smaller pair?

What's happening?
See page 74.

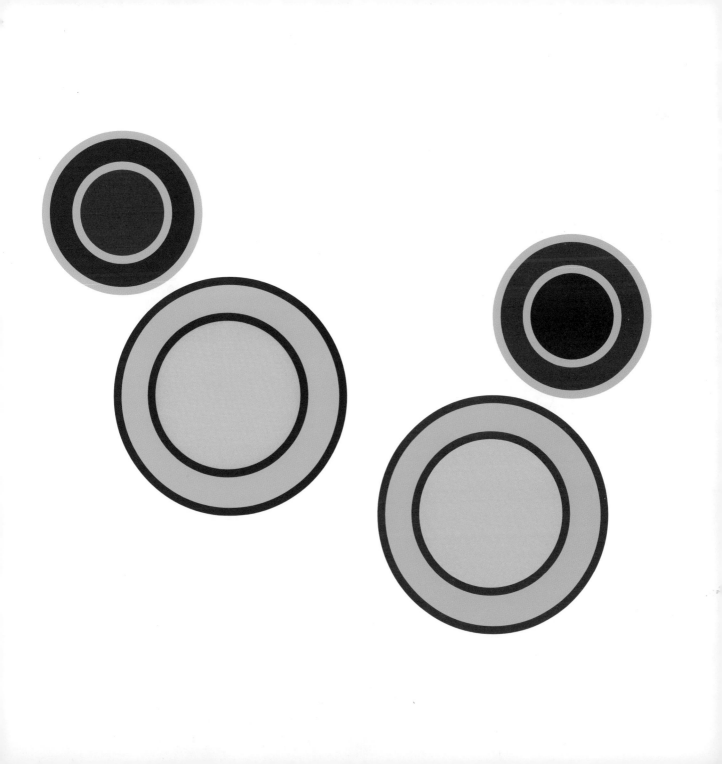

End of the Tunnel

Are the inside squares the same size from figure to figure?

Are the smallest squares exactly in the center?

Are the background colors the same in each figure?

Do the sides of any of the boxes change colors?

What's happening?
See page 75.

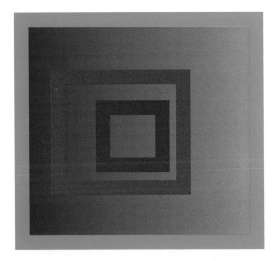

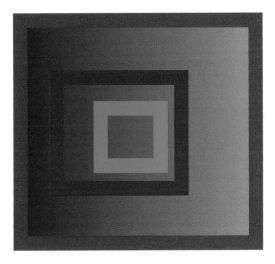

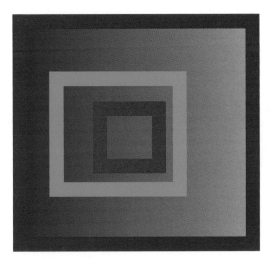

Barrel Roll

Do the circle groups appear as two-dimensional circles or three-dimensional barrels?

In Figure A, does the left or right circle in each group seem closest to you?

In Figure B, what changes when the colors in each group are different?

What's happening?
See page 75.

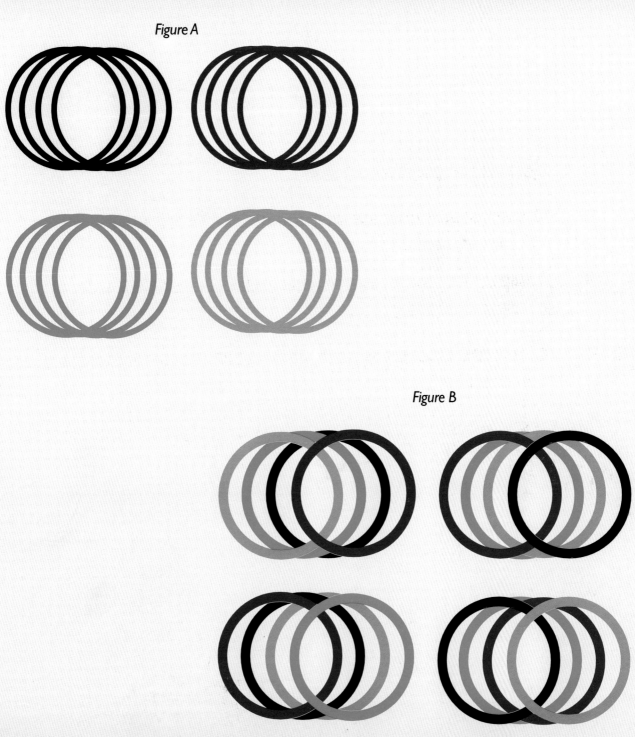

Figure A

Figure B

Bending Bridges

Which of the four colored lines in the middle are straight?

Which ones are curved?

What's happening?
See page 76.

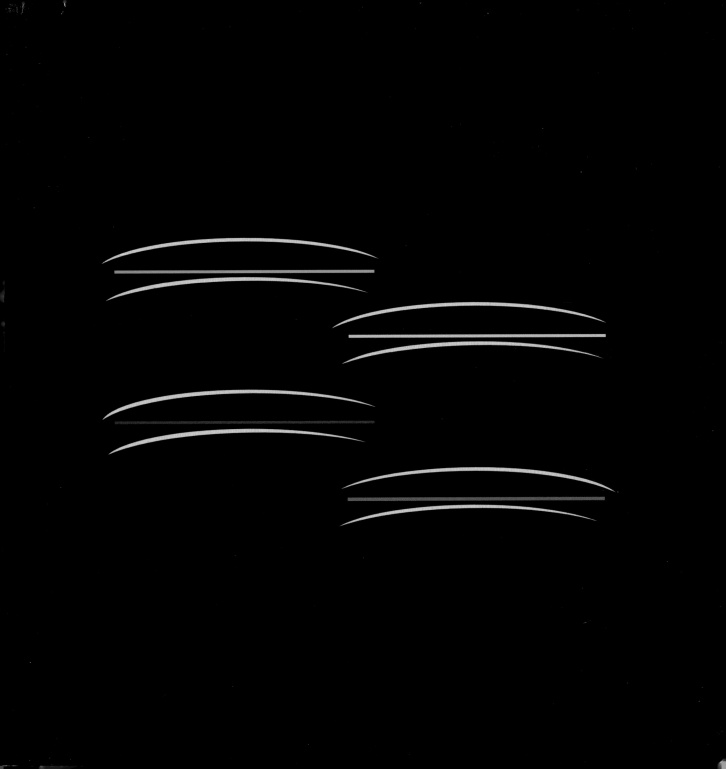

Midnight Sun

Which is larger, the star on the left or the red sun
in the center?

Is the red of the sun glowing brighter than the star?

How many kinds of shapes are on this page?

What's happening?
See page 76.

Amazing Grays

Each "W" is made from smaller bars.

Are all the number 1 bars the same color?

Are all the number 2 bars the same color?

Are all the number 3 bars the same color?

What's happening?
See page 77.

Figure A

2

1

Figure B

3
2
1

Figure C

3

2

Spaghetti Machine

How many different colors are on this page?

What's happening?
See page 77.

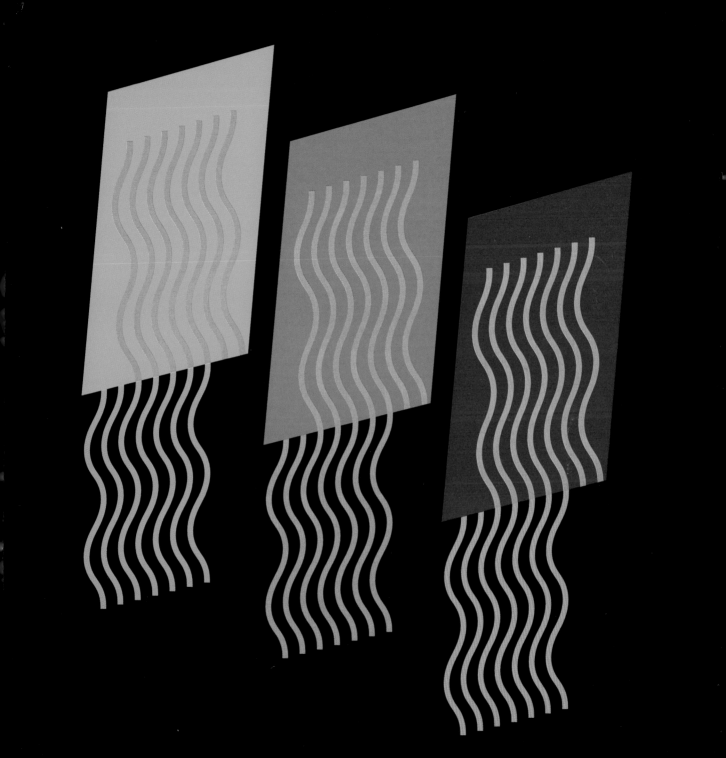

Circles and Triangles

Look at the very center between the four circles.

How many kinds of shapes are on this page?

Do any of the circles change color?

What's happening?
See page 78.

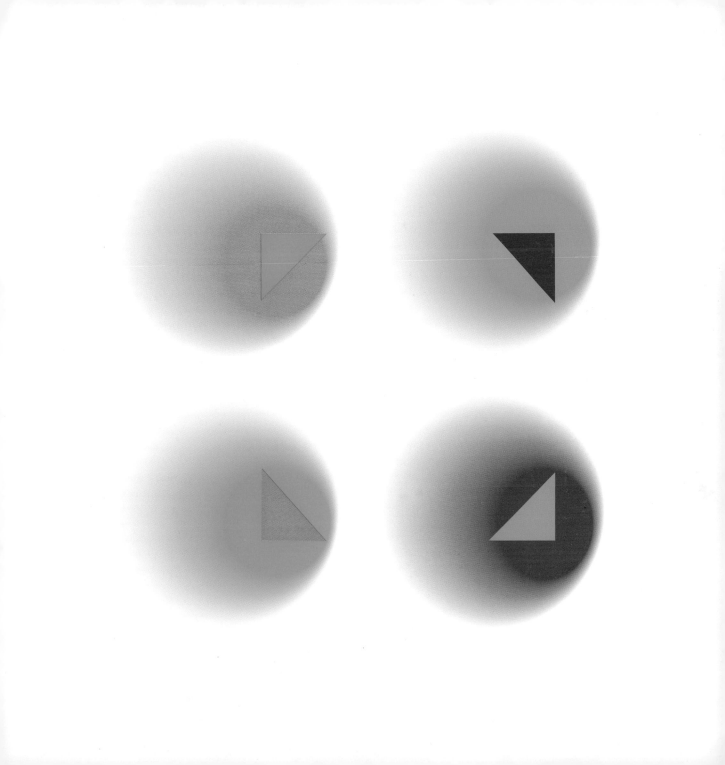

WHAT'S HAPPENING?

The highlighted terms are explained on pages 78 and 79.

Narrow Arrows

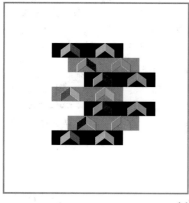

page 16

WHAT'S HAPPENING:

The arrows on black probably appear to point upward.
The black background makes the complementary colors appear lighter and brighter, so they come forward.

The arrows on gray probably appear to point downward.
The gray background is closer in value to the arrows.
That makes them look flatter and pushes them back.

If you look at the entire illusion together, the arrows may seem to shift back and forth.
That's because these two effects conflict.
This is called the principle of good continuation.

True Blue?

page 18

WHAT'S HAPPENING:

Both sets of blue bars are exactly the same color.
On a blue diamond, the blue bars fizzle and strike out. But put them in front of a red diamond and they fly right out of the field. This effect comes from simultaneous contrast.

3 Sides, 3 Corners, 3D

WHAT'S HAPPENING:

These Penrose Triangles are a pure optical illusion. They cannot be built.

When Mr. Penrose designed these seemingly 3D triangles, he knew they couldn't exist in real space. Follow one side around the corner, and it impossibly becomes a different side at a completely different angle. These triangles seem to exist in three places at the same time.

In color, the triangles can become less confusing.

The colored triangles in the last panel look less like illusions and more like designs. Because black and gray give an illusion of shadows, the triangles in the middle panel have more contrast. They become more dimensional—more "realistic"—and so the brain struggles harder to make sense of them.

The triangles aren't really tumbling.

You see the triangles aiming downward in a familiar, clockwise manner. Your mind fills in the blanks and completes the story.

TV Dinner

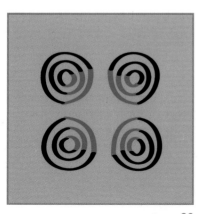

WHAT'S HAPPENING:

The orange background does not change color.

Because it is surrounded by light blue on all sides, the orange in the middle gives the sensation of becoming more blue. At the same time, the orange makes the blue edges seem even more blue than they are.

There are only circles on this page.

You may think you see a light blue square, which looks like the reflection of a TV set. But it isn't really there. The principle of closure makes your mind put the edges together to form a shape.

Dots and Diamonds

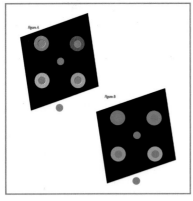

page 24

WHAT'S HAPPENING:

Within each diamond, all the dots are exactly the same color.
The six gray dots in Figure A appear to be different, for two reasons: simultaneous contrast and the afterimage effect. As a result, the dots appear lighter, darker, pinker, bluer, and so on. This illusion is also true in Figure B.

All the center dots match the dot outside the diamond.
The outside dots are the original colors. See how much they change when the rings around them change? In fact, the only dots that don't match are the groups in Figures A and B. But you probably figured that out.

Dandelions

page 26

WHAT'S HAPPENING:

Each double dandelion appears to blend into a single one.
You may have to stand back and squint, but eventually your eyes will blend the two dandelions together.

When a double dandelion blends, it creates the color of its partner.
The colors in each double dandelion are mixed together inside your head, until each matches the color of its next-door neighbor. Each single color—the violet, the red, and the green—is made from the two hues in its double-dandelion partner.

Stick Matches

page 28

WHAT'S HAPPENING:

There are eight gray sticks on this page.
Look closely. Your brain is so eager to connect the sticks that it's willing to ignore how they come together. Because they don't. The red circles at the end of each bar—and **the law of proximity**—do their tricks, so you see four sticks.

Wavy Groovy

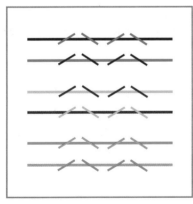

page 30

WHAT'S HAPPENING:

All the horizontal bars are straight and parallel.
That means none of the bars are wavy. But they're groovy.

Which color bars appear more wavy? That's up to you.
The horizontal bars look wavy, thanks to the slanted lines on top. Each pair of slants and bars has contrasting **hues** that are in **harmony**. This makes the bars look brighter at those intersections, and that's why they appear wavy.

Whirly Swirly

page 32

WHAT'S HAPPENING:

All the outside circles in each figure are the same distance from each other.
On a dark background, the bright colors appear farther apart and the dark colors appear closer together. The dark background also makes colors appear lighter or brighter, no matter what their hue or brightness.

The largest and smallest circles are all true circles.
But with all those ovals in between, the eyes get confused.

To most people, the circles appear to be moving.
The difference is all about how the loops fit together. In Figure A, each set of loops appears to be rotating within itself. In Figure B, all the loops rotate as a unit. Your eye follows these loops continuously… clockwise… until either they're spinning, or your eyes are.

Box of Dots

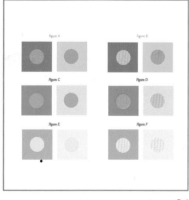

page 34

WHAT'S HAPPENING:

Figures A, B, C, and F have dots that match in the middle.
Simultaneous contrast between the different colored squares and the dots make the inside dots look different when they're really the same.

Figures D and E have mismatched gray dots in the middle.
The colors of the squares in D and E may make the dots appear more similar than they are. But they don't match. This is the *opposite* use of simultaneous contrast. Isn't dot amazing?

White Triangles

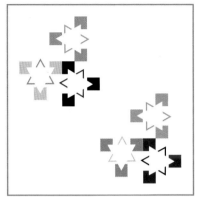

page 36

WHAT'S HAPPENING:

There are no squares.
Squares have four sides.

There are no triangles.
Triangles have three sides.

No shape is on top of another.
Shape? What shape? You can see for yourself. It's an *illusion*. But to most people, the "white triangle" appears to be on top, blocking part of the lines on the "colored triangle."

The "white triangles" seem to be affected by the different colors surrounding them.
When surrounded by black and gray shapes, the imaginary triangles appear bright. When the shapes have brighter colors, the imaginary triangles appear duller. **Simultaneous contrast** strikes again.

Bars and Stripes Forever

page 38

WHAT'S HAPPENING:

There are no transparent bars.
Although the bars are different shades of blue, none are actually transparent. First the blue vertical bars interact together. Then the black and white surrounding them help the bars to go back and come forward at the same time. The result should be transparent to everyone.

There are four white bars.
The rest are not bars—they don't have two ends. Thanks to **the law of similarity**, the white color becomes a shape under the bars, but it is really just the space in between the bars.

No bar is in front of another.
They are all next to each other.

Red Grill

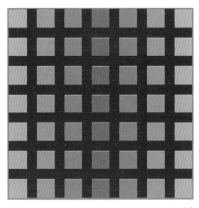

page 40

WHAT'S HAPPENING:

The green boxes change color.
They are lighter at the sides, and grow darker toward the center.

The red lines do not change color.
The red grill gives the perception of shifting from dark to light as the outer edges move toward the center. The darker middle squares cause this to happen. Simultaneous contrast creates the glowing effect you see.

Are you seeing spots before your eyes?
Don't panic. While looking at large grids, the eyes often see gray dots where the lines cross.

Whether you see red on green or green on red is up to you.
Look at it long enough and you'll probably see it both ways.

Fact Checkers

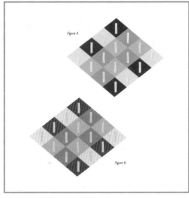

page 42

from
Figure B

from
Figure A

WHAT'S HAPPENING:

All the small vertical lines are the same width.
Objects look thinner when their background makes them look darker.

The lines in the black and red fields are different colors.
The lines are actually as different as the blue and gray patches below. On the black background, all the lines are blue-green and they don't change color. On the red background, the lines are really gray. But they look blue-green. Simultaneous contrast makes both sets of lines seem like the same color.

Dashing Dots

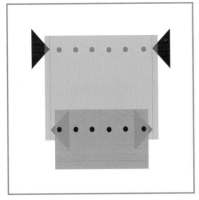

page 44

WHAT'S HAPPENING:

On both lines of dots, the space between dots is the same.
In this illusion the blue dots appear wider apart than the red ones.
The dots look like they're *s-t-r-e-t-c-h-e-d* between red triangles that are farther away in the larger box.

Both lines of dots are the same length.
This visual-geometric illusion, by Mueller–Lyer, is easy once you know it. There are three different effects that make the line of red dots look closer together. The bottom triangles are turned around, crowding the red dots with their long sides. The triangles cover two of the dots. And the smaller, lower box crowds the dots even more. This is the principle of good continuation in action.

Mountains by Satellite

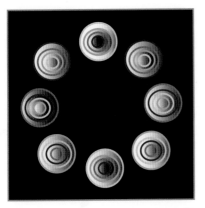

page 46

WHAT'S HAPPENING:

None of the inside rings change size or position.
There are only three different sizes of inside rings, and all eight versions are the same. The gray shadows make some rings appear to shift, but they don't.

If you see the mountains, they probably seem like different heights.
Each mountain has different amounts of shadowing, which helps you see them as "high" or "low." Changing the locations of the red rings also increases this effect, thanks to the principle of closure.

And it's very likely they appear to be in motion.
The circles seem to vibrate in and out in different ways. Sometimes the centers go backward, sometimes they go forward. And when you turn the page, they go away.

Stilts Tilts

page 48

WHAT'S HAPPENING:

Each of the vertical lines is perfectly parallel.
This is the well-known Zoellner effect. The vertical parallel lines give the **sensation** of converging (coming together) and diverging (moving apart) at the same time.

Each line is straight.
The crossing lines help with the effect of converging and diverging. This is no way to paint a road.

Crazy Eights

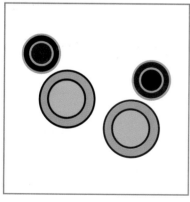

page 50

WHAT'S HAPPENING:

The inside and outside rings are the same size.
The outer rings of the smaller circles and the inner rings of the larger circles are equal. But one is part of a bigger circle and the other is part of a smaller circle. **The law of proximity** tricks us into seeing the circles inside the bigger circles as bigger than they are. But they're not.

Both large circles are the same size. So are the smaller ones.
In both cases, the circles with blue on the outside look smaller than the circles with red on the outside because of red's darker **value**.

End of the Tunnel

page 52

WHAT'S HAPPENING:

The inside squares do not change size from figure to figure.
Sometimes the green square appears to be bigger. Don't let this alarm you.

The smallest squares are not centered.
They sit to the left of center. Sometimes you have to believe your eyes.

The background colors in all three are exactly the same.
Maybe the different colored boxes fooled you, especially because the background has a floating effect on the boxes in the middle. This is a classic example of simultaneous contrast.

The border on each box always stays the same color.
Because the background shifts from light to dark, it affects how the colored lines look. The sides may appear brighter or lighter—fading into the background—or darker, bluer, yellower, or redder simultaneously. But that's all in your head. For extra zip, trace your eyes along the sides of each box and see what happens.

Barrel Roll

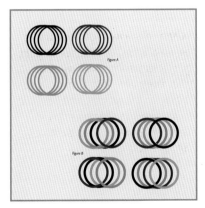

page 54

WHAT'S HAPPENING:

For many, the circle groups seem to make the shape of a barrel.
The law of similarity says that our minds naturally take similar objects and group them together.

Stare long enough, and the barrels shift from one side to another.
Something that seems to change direction and reverse, depending on your point of view, is called a reversible figure.

When the circles are different colors, your eyes become confused.
The colored circle groups in Figure B seem to break the law of similarity. Your eyes want to make them into barrels, but the effect of the colors keeps them shifting back and forth.

Bending Bridges

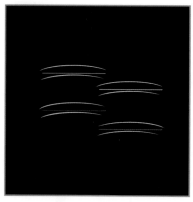

page 56

WHAT'S HAPPENING:

All of the middle lines are straight and parallel.
The horizontal lines appear to be bending downward in the middle and upward toward the ends. This phenomenon is created by the closeness of the curved lines to the center of the straight lines, and also by how close the ends of the straight lines are to the curves.

Midnight Sun

page 58

WHAT'S HAPPENING:

The red star and the red sun are exactly the same size.
The large black lines give the illusion that the sun's red part is also larger. But they're the same size.

The red color of the sun and the star are the same.
The red on the sun appears brighter because it sits against the black rays. There is simultaneous contrast between the black and the red—so the black makes the red appear both lighter and brighter.

There is only one kind of shape on this page.
Call it a star. Call it a snowflake. Call it an asterisk. But don't call anything a circle. The red sun appears to be round because your mind wants to fill in the missing parts and make it seem whole. If you see a circle, you're a victim of the law of proximity.

Amazing Grays

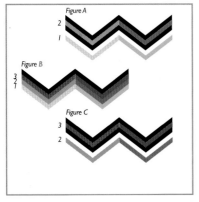

page 60

WHAT'S HAPPENING:

Each bar matches the other bars with the same numbers.
The three different shades of gray (1, 2, and 3) are switched around, surrounded by total black or total white. This gives them the illusion of appearing to be the same. They look different because of their juxtaposition against the white and black bars. Look at bar 2 in Figure A. Look at how it appears to be as light as the gray bar 1 in Figure B, and as dark as the gray bar 3 in Figure C.

Spaghetti Machine

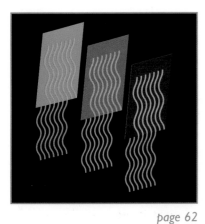

page 62

WHAT'S HAPPENING:

There are seven different colors on this page.
Each spaghetti machine makes spaghetti that is its complementary color. And when you blend two complementary colors, you get gray. In this illusion, the spaghetti are different colors at the bottom. But inside each machine, they are all *the exact same gray*. So how many colors are there? You have three different-colored spaghetti machines, three different flavors of spaghetti, and the same gray color inside every machine. So your total is seven. (Remember, black isn't a color—it's the *absence* of color!)

inside all machines

outside each machine

Circles and Triangles

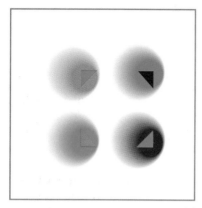

page 64

WHAT'S HAPPENING:

There are two kinds of shapes on this page.

There are circles and triangles. You see a square? That illusion comes from the way those four triangles sit next to each other. You see the corners, so you imagine the sides of a square. Those invisible sides are called subjective contours.

None of the circles change color.

The circles appear to be lighter on one side and darker on the other. But they're not. Imagine that each circle is made from a million little dots, all the same color. The dots on the "lighter" side are just farther apart, and you see white in between them. On the "darker" side, the dots are closer together, so you can't see the white. The colors in each of these four circles have the maximum in brightness. To help this effect, the complementary colors of the triangles were chosen to make them appear to float, as if they were popping off the page.

FOUR RULES

How your mind sees things

The law of proximity

Things that are close to one another tend to be seen as one single thing.
(Example: *Stick Matches,* page 69)

The law of similarity

Things that are similar tend to be grouped together.
(Example: *Barrel Roll,* page 75)

The principle of closure

Spaces and areas that are surrounded by items or sides are easily seen as shapes and figures.
(Example: *Circles and Triangles,* above)

The principle of good continuation

Things that seem to follow in the same direction tend to be grouped together.
(Example: *Narrow Arrows,* page 66)

GLOSSARY

Afterimage
An afterimage is an effect that happens to your eyes. Often when you look at a light and then turn away, the image stays in your eyes for a short time and you can still see it. This can happen with colors, too. When you focus on one color, the afterimage effect immediately makes its opposite, complementary color appear in front of your eyes. When two complementary colors are put next to each other, they affect each other and both look brighter.
(Example: *Dots and Diamonds,* page 68)

Brightness
When there's less gray in a color, there's more brightness. When there's no gray at all, the color is pure, or fully "saturated."
(Example: *Whirly Swirly,* page 70)

Complementary colors
Colors that are complementary are exact opposites that work together. When they're mixed together, you get gray. Red/green, blue/orange, and yellow/violet are among the pairs of complementary colors.
(Example: *Spaghetti Machine,* page 77)

Contrast
The contrast between colors is measured by their differences, based on qualities such as value and brightness. The most contrast comes from black (which has no color) and white (which contains the most light).
(Example: *True Blue?,* page 66)

Harmony
Colors that are complementary are said to be in harmony with each other. When you mix colors that are in harmony, you get gray. And that's how the gray Manx (on page 3) got his name.
(Example: *Wavy Groovy,* page 69)

Hue
This is another word for color.
(Example: *Dandelions,* page 68)

Juxtaposition
When you put objects or colors side by side in order to compare them, you juxtapose them.
(Example: *Amazing Grays,* page 77)

Perceive/Perception
When you see something, your mind reacts in its own special way. What you *think* you see is called perception. You and someone else can look at the same thing and perceive it two different ways. That's because you both have your own unique perceptions.
(Example: *Red Grill,* page 72)

Sensation
When you react to something using any of your five senses, you are having a sensation.
(Example: *TV Dinner,* page 67)

Simultaneous contrast
All colors affect each other when they are next to each other. Simultaneous contrast makes each one look different than it really is. When this happens, you get the afterimage effect.
(Example: *Box of Dots,* page 70)

Subjective contours
When your mind perceives sides and edges that are not really there, it is seeing subjective contours.
(Example: *White Triangles,* page 71)

Value
This is how you describe the darkness or the lightness of a color.
(Example: *Narrow Arrows,* page 66)

INDEX